strange land

Crab Orchard Series in Poetry

Open Competition Award

T0164613

strange land

TODD HEARON

Crab Orchard Review

&

Southern Illinois University Press

CARBONDALE AND EDWARDSVILLE

13 12 11 10   4 3 2 1

The Crab Orchard Series in Poetry is a joint publishing venture of
Southern Illinois University Press and *Crab Orchard Review*. This
series has been made possible by the generous support of the Office
of the President of Southern Illinois University and the Office of
the Vice Chancellor for Academic Affairs and Provost at Southern
Illinois University Carbondale.

Crab Orchard Series in Poetry Editor: Jon Tribble
Open Competition Award Judge for 2009: Natasha Trethewey

Library of Congress Cataloging-in-Publication Data

Hearon, Todd, 1968–
     Strange land / Todd Hearon.
         p. cm. — (Crab Orchard series in poetry)
     Includes bibliographical references.
     ISBN-13: 978-0-8093-2966-3 (pbk. : alk. paper)
     ISBN-10: 0-8093-2966-2 (pbk. : alk. paper)
     ISBN-13: 978-0-8093-8568-3 (ebook)
     ISBN-10: 0-8093-8568-6 (ebook)

     I. Title.
PS3608.E266S77   2010
811'.6—dc22   2009029389

Printed on recycled paper. ♻

The paper used in this publication meets the minimum
requirements of American National Standard for Information
Sciences—Permanence of Paper for Printed Library Materials,
ANSI Z39.48-1992. ∞

For Maggie, fellow traveler

These all died in faith, not having received the promises, but having seen them afar off, and were persuaded of them, and embraced them, and confessed that they were strangers and pilgrims on the earth. For they that say such things declare plainly that they seek a country.

—Hebrews 11:13–14

How shall we sing the Lord's song in a strange land?

—Psalm 137:4

Contents

Acknowledgments

The author would like to thank the editors of the following journals, in whose pages these poems originally appeared:

AGNI—"Covenant" and "Song for the Returns"
Harvard Review—"Sea Change" (under the title "The Death of Shelley")
Literary Imagination—"Dantescan Fragment" and "In Those Days"
Memorious—"De Profundis," "Harry Farr," "Sundial," and "Translation"
The New Republic—"Suppliant, Late April"
Partisan Review—"Caliban in After-Life"
Ploughshares—"Ancestors" and "Atlantis"
Poetry—"After the President's Speech You Dream of Corpses," "Roman Room," "The Singers," and "Voyager"
Poetry Ireland Review—"Clothing for the Transformation" (under the title "Pilgrimage")
Poetry London—"Last Look"
Salamander—"After the Flood" and "World's End"
Sea Change—"Song for the Interstices"
Slate—"What Is Man That Thou Art Mindful of Him"
The Sleepers Almanac No. 5—"To Childhood"

"Last Look" was republished on *Verse Daily* (www.versedaily.org), January 27, 2008.

"Ancestors," "The Singers," and "What Is Man That Thou Art Mindful of Him" were reprinted in *Enskyment: An Anthology of Print and Online Poetry*.

"Atlantis" was published by Boston's Firefly Press in a limited edition broadside designed by Bruce Kennett.

Thanks to Andrea Cohen, David Ferry, Eamon Grennan, Eric Ormsby, Robert Pinsky, Christopher Ricks, Don Share, Dan Tobin, Natasha Trethewey, and Rosanna Warren for their good faith, encouragement, and support. Thanks to Maggie Dietz for everything—and for everything else.

Ann Miller, in memoriam
The piller pearisht is whearto I lent

strange land

Dantescan Fragment

And I came in my dream to the base of that mountain
no longer believed in, no more feared, no more desired
to where the sea lay frozen, wave on wave, a flower

transparent in its intricacies and wrapped in silence
and I saw along its shore lay many birds, gulls, sparrows
also frozen, I found, as I picked one (like a flower)

and held it openthroated in my palm, small
wren, it seemed, but there were no longer any names
the names were elsewhere, as I understood

to say *wren sparrow gull* even *flower*
next to that sea was not to be endured
inside that house of silence, the glass waves.

And I saw that the sun had dropped from heaven
and it shone up through the petals of the sea
and the fire of creation was a rose

untellable in beauty but to speak

one

Ancestors

The shadow of a wasp
swung like a pendulum, back and forth
across the kitchen table in the light of five
o'clock where seven loaves were steaming.

It was the past, could have been many pasts.
I recognized it gradually as mine.
Besides, the dead that sat around the table were mine
and rose to make me welcome.

It was not as it is written
in almanac or album: ash-
thin, they were not wasted
but bright and hale.

The madness, the bad blood had gone.
Here were the gracious accents, all
the old talk, crops, children.
Here were the hands of snow.

I sat down, we all sat down together.
One offered grace, I saw the fingers fall
over the loaves that never can be broken
though they be shattered, pulled apart as loves.

To Childhood

Moth-eaten faith, old flame (old shame) I have sworn
you off. Again. To furtively return—
bourbon I stashed in the basement mattress where
my uncle whoops it up with country whores:

> You are no good to me
> if I continue to abuse you.
> Why can't I let you die?
> You've done your chores.

Your fishbowl full of formaldehyde,
your toy box rupturing with foreign wars—
no one believes you, childhood.
Let alone my poems.

> But at night the lost limb itches.

I follow you down my Florida of the mind,
poor Ponce de León, after his beloved,
syphilitic guide.

Sundial

Once as a child and only once I walked
into the past time of their making, those godlike ones

so unappeasable so separate at one
in a tangle of sunlight on the riddled sheets.

She lay, open to my knowing. On her belly,
bare, his finger played. And the branch

of its shadow foundered to a darker shade
moss damp and pearled with honey.

I closed the door. The time was one o'clock
I noted on the garden sundial's face

following its triangle of dark
down from the gnomon to the *I* engraved.

The Singers

They are not angels

though they have the hollow look

of beings bred on ether. There's an air

of cool removal from your life, the hawk's

indifference to the hare's terror.

You see it in their palms, raised casually

against the fresco surface, as to glass

of submarine or spacecraft, and you see

it in their eyes, oracular, that let you pass

alone to unknown agony. The song

they sing is merely time.

Harry Farr

Executed by firing squad, 1916, after refusing
to return to the trenches

And as the intimate bullet enters
the kerchief pinned and fluttering at my breast
white as a moth, ich innocent, I shall think

of the stars that doomed me, amniotic flecks,
flint-castings harrowing at dawn the iron
shell I cannot enter, cannot enter ever

again. For hear me, I was born
too far from beauty and have always been
away, a child who sought in soundless things,

painted butterfly or spotted mole,
the soul of beauty. They eluded me.
Man was the destiny I fell to, do not call

it fear that I refuse to put it on. Once
I knocked I heard the clicking shut
of doors down corridors forever. Hell

is like that. You can hear it in the dawn
in the dark disconsolate labyrinthine scream
of shells my memory's almost become.

Hell is the echo of a quiet I dreamed
that haunts me nightly, dogs me as a child
will dog his mother's shadow. Now we speak

of shades. I am becoming one with time,
the rifles cocked, my brothers in a line
like ripening corn—all ears, all ears—

I pity them. Would I were not the cause.
I would not add to this eternity of noise.

In Those Days

> To have lived is not enough for them . . .
> To be dead is not enough for them.
>
> —Beckett

Light reared its glassine house

and onion skin of hours we looked through
as through a soap filmed pane
on frost encrusted fields.

So we inhabited ourselves
as strangers, eyes trained to a lighted screen

in Plato's cave
                    day's images
flickering on our brows and chins—

lust and conquest, a single severed breast
floating by like the face of Orpheus
his lips a nipple pursed on the remembered

consequence of song.

Was this the day that our desire had made?
Was this its end? Those evenings we burned down
with oil and camphor, leaving not an ash—

What matter.
                    Dawn would raise them up again
in tall translucent panels

as though they had been peeled from our own skin.

Song for the Returns

Before our bodies were the bodies
we innocently call our own, or more

innocently still the bodies that we seek
to give in love, as *I am yours* or *I in you*

inhabit my desire, although desire
only so long as left unsatisfied, O what

to call that place when all desire was
gone, a conflagration through the roof

as we lay empty, dispossessed, at one
with the ashes of this house, my phoenix?

Atlantis

About that country there's not much left to say.
Blue sun, far off, a watery vein
in the cloud belt. The solid earth itself
unremarkable: familiar ruins
littered with standing stones our people
had lost the ability to decipher.
How deeply had we slept? Beneath the jellyfish
umbels of evergreens, each one a dream,
and the effervescent stars, cold currents
tugged at our thoughts like tapestries
unraveling into war. All spring
the nightingale perched on the green volcano's lip.
The rats had abandoned the temples.
My mind was a voyage hungering to happen.

Strange Land

It goes without saying
a word: the world under cover
of midnight snow, what we have known

of pageantry and lilac, leaf and song
subsumed in starless silence.
Waking at dawn into the tremulous blue

of the room, as in earth's afterglow,
we lie, lidless, listening, as crows
call out the ear's horizons.

What year is it? Into what country were we born
and now must make our way? Outside the pane
the stillness feels ancestral but the ghosts

not yours, not mine. My émigré,
we are cut off. An ocean to the east
churns in chiaroscuro while unseen

ranges to the south deflect our passage,
what passage might have been.
This country seems the passing of a dream

to a moonscape's still immitigable white,
a land's amnesia where against the sky
three needling black birds fly

and slip like an ellipsis out of sight.

two

Last Look

The ice caps of Greenland and Antarctica are melting but
the Neolithic Briton had a one-in-fourteen chance

of having his head bashed in. What do you do
with the mass grave of dodos discovered on Mauritius, with

the family of retarded people walking on all fours
they found in Turkey? Either you get up or you don't

and scientists insist we're still evolving. A recent
study of bats found that males with big brains have

small testicles. Holocaust survivors are more prone
to die from cancer. Guppies go through menopause. The rhesus

monkey drinks more when it drinks alone. Homesickness
is on the rise in Canada. A pair of inebriated moose attacked

a Swedish old folks' home. So what they did
in Guantánamo was shocking but not really

more than Taiwan's transgenic pigs that glow
in the dark—as, apparently, so do we—or the toxic

waste in the Arctic turning hungry polar bears
hermaphroditic. It's extreme, but the gene

experts conjecture we're only about ten percent
human, the rest of our cells bacteria. And the red

rains that fell mysteriously over India back
in 2001, no one knows what they were.

Astronomers posit small clusters of galaxies near
Andromeda are floating on a "river of dark

matter" and think Pluto to be
colder than Charon, its moon. We're not alone:

dolphins use names and songbirds
grammar. The male Nigerian putty-nosed

monkey makes the sentence *pyow hack hack pyow
hack hack* to indicate it's time to be moving on.

What Is Man That Thou Art Mindful of Him

Man is a weapon of mass destruction.
Eliminate man you don't eliminate
the Problem. As dog to its own filth, so man returns

a swarm, a fungus, feeding on destruction—
as when a child I fed upon my dreams
adrift in a pool rainbowed with chemicals

a child already dead, intent on death.
Think of the thousands I marshaled to destruction
five hundred years, having fed upon the earth

(there is no better rhyme with death than earth)—
I tore the heart from Montezuma's bride.
I saw Bikini as a nippled blast.

Moon rises at moth rise. I dream a jungle
from my fruitless cot. I dream my father
spidering the walls of the house in anger.

I think back to my mother. I think
I was a man, born on earth of woman.
Woman is a weapon of mass destruction.

I sleep. I dream my feudal fruitless wars.
I dream of peace the dovewhite dawn explodes.
Man is a weapon of mass destruction.
I know this now. Man's the best rhyme for war.

De Profundis

What we have not heard
will never help us. What we have not seen
by now will never save. The city

drowned under winter sunlight like a bad
migraine, the bars shut down,
hint of a pandemic in the air, in wind

invisible, the guess and gust of wings.
The pigeons have come home to die.
There are corpses floating in the trees.

2

There are corpses floating in the trees.
High clouds roll over as on holiday.
The sun, impassive as a president,

palters for time and tide. Once we could pray
with honest hunger for whatever life
drew from its magician's hat;

now rabbits sicken on the mutant vine
and hunger is our habitat.
We are hungry. We have never been so hungry.

3

What we have not followed
leads us now. What follows is a thing we never
dreamed. Prisoners storm the empty coliseum.

In its cage, the gaunt heart screams.
Beneath ground, gears and levers
issue another victim to the light.

The trapdoor opens: thunder
erupts like anesthetic through the night.
The bars swing open. We have all gone under.

After the Flood

We wondered, being human, what we'd done
to deserve it, even then not comprehending
the hubris in assuming something
human at the root. The skies

opened. That was all.
A wall of water fell. If it had been
our judgment we'd have judged it at the least
sufficient. It was not.

So dead we are returned
as rain to tell you all
we ascertained too late:
the earth was not enough.

World's End

So to return to that sun-drenched skeleton of land, my love, and find
nothing more evident, no less elusive than it was before: monotonous
    wind

pulled across ailing embers in a bumfuck ditch
the sea seeps in, a mess of clothes and feathers, bones and such

dunes. The dunes' sparse winter grasses.
White sand striated by the stylus trace

of crab- or turtle claw, through which we move
again like tourists on the outmost groove

of a Zen garden discovered in the wilderness—
nothing to dwell on, nothing to express.

And still the high-flung hammering of gulls,
still the mollusk wrenched into its shivering pool,

pools among the rocks, rocks along a coast that cooled
an age ago, upon a different Earth: a world

of fire and frenzy, what a ball it was,
come down to coals the wind picks over. Us.

After the President's Speech You Dream of Corpses

Those bodies that last night
stormed the bosses in your brain
—some picket-line or strike—
and were beaten down
so brutally, batoned
corpses piled the streets,
men and women, naked,
massive, Blakean physiques:
where are they now?
                    Anonymous,
shoveled in the mass
grave your mind's become
at morning after dream.
So you are the mirror
of your times: a century
rots forgotten, storyless
in you. Sepulcher, articulate
and ambulating tomb. Packed
charnel house. Dead to the very eyes.

Where will you be that morning when they rise?

Caliban in After-Life

> . . . this thing of darkness I
> Acknowledge mine.

Prospero, what hollow art
makes human humane?
Excepting one, I can accept
the other. Neither a
deity nor its dog sits
court upon a question of
this sort. So answer,
Sorcerer. Conqueror,
I wait.

Wordless as I was when you
washed up heaving brine, in
ignorance of pity I
pitied you, thin thing
the salt had scoured. Dry,
you wept then slept the ocean out
of mind. When it returned,
I nested you, laid you in
my lair.
       So was it there,
sequestered, out of thirst
your tongue put forth my first-
heard word?
          Water
What sun could sear,
what sea-roar will erase
its acid from my ear?

Your daughter's laughter
as I played the pup,
lapping berries from her open
fist?—that, Master, was the best
relish I had had since Mother's milk.
And last. For it, too, found a word
in your dread lexicon:
lubricious. Admonished,
Miranda wandered off. The dog
days ceased. All moon
I went on wanting.

Prospero, before you the lagoon
wombed me. Reedy light
sifted me, in dreams I lay
unnamed, alluvial sprite.
Beside the tidepools I'd
bask in the unasked
unconscious Question,
fathomless in spite
of worlds turned upwards underhand—
that now turn all against me: my
face at every surface
surfeits on its own, grown
overmonstrous, even
my moon half-man.
My bellow crawls through cliffs,
outchoirs the sea's echo:
CALIBAN CANIBAL
I gnaw myself, I know.

If you can hear me, Master,
mustering music on this crust
of land, this isle
I'll always lie alien on now,
float home, my sometime father,

some grain of grace to scour
my skull of ill, its misery,
my memory. One ounce
of the old art, Alchemist, one
phial's drop to prosper o-
blivion
in Caliban
in language languishing.

You drowned your book and sailed.
Your chief achieve remains
my curse: You worded me;
I can't recant my life.

Translation

1

As if a god washed up.
  As if a god
out of the blue, fin-winged,
  its great horse head
  wreathed with dark weed

2

and the men came with tools
  as if for slaughter
hacked at the meat, tossed back
  upon the water
  's receding laughter

3

buried the bones in dung
  the precious bone
let maggots have their say
  out of the sun
  for a season

4

dug up, scraped clean, boiled down
  removing all
memory of flesh, sinew,
  the vital oil
  from spine and skull

5

and the men made a rod
    the women spun
into a helix curve
    and strung the spine
    like pearls upon

6

it, so when hoisted up
    vertically through
the sunlit atrium's
    rippling blue
    for all to view

7

it seemed a thing of grace,
    it seemed a thing
swam over us in flight,
    imagining
    the bone white wing.

Psalm

I

       An echo seeking out the voice that sent it

have I sought for you who are

       intimate as air the listener's breath

catches in the cavern's mouth

       when I imagine you have made my name

              ring out

in darkness back through dark

       to gather me and draw me in

the silence where my stillness says

       you swim

2

Pardon my presumption I want to live

    forever

as everyone does once

    not granting your last grace may be

death enough to die eternally

What a hell we've made of earth forgive us

What a hell made of each other

The hubris

        to have failed at life

to hope to fail at death

.

3

But if as it is said there is to be

      another Earth a second heaven

and men move through it as in days of old

      stalwart rejoicing

O unrestrict your will

      unlike you have done

so mercifully with us

            to let us choose

      impassively

            resignedly our own

annihilation

Why when we cracked did you not shatter us

and start anew

      another Earth a second heaven

if what they say is true

4

Others have praised you that you are

    unattributable

        which is only to assign

you yet another attribute

           I say

nothing but wait by day by night

till the nothing that you are be blotted out

5

Forgive me my vanishing that most of all

    I presumed to be of durable use

your words in my voice your works in my hand

    in ignorance and arrogance I bore

forward only error

                but let that lie

And let me dwell in the dark of your memory forever

three

Sea Change

> I have a boat here. It cost me £80 and reduced me to
> some difficulty in point of money. However, it is swift
> and beautiful, and appears quite a vessel. Williams
> is captain, and we drive along this delightful bay in
> the evening wind under the summer moon until earth
> appears another world. Jane brings her guitar, and if the
> past and future could be obliterated, the present would
> content me so well that I could say with Faust to the
> passing moment 'Remain thou, thou art so beautiful.'
> —Shelley, letter to John Gisborne, June 19, 1822

1. Vortex

Gulf of Spezia, Via Reggio
August 14, 1822

We were startled and drawn together
by a dull hollow sound that followed the blow
of the mattock. The iron had struck a skull.

Soldiers loitered in the shade, dark horses.
Some collected fuel, dry planks and spars
cast up from earlier wrecks

(one played
pieces of a ballad on a pine guitar)

as we assembled
the iron bars and sheet-iron of the pyre
shipped in for the occasion.

Along the edges of a stunted pine
forest, the spectators were gathering,
among them many ladies, richly dressed.

2. *Tempest*

Casa Magni, San Terenzo
May 12, 1822

Then, as we stared into the gloaming light,
orange water and the low majestic wrack
of clouds,
         the day's dust lifted off the mountain olives
settling on the water in a lime-green haze,
                   across the bay,
along the boundary of the outmost rocks—
at first a concentration of the rocks
in cormorant-sharpness, rigid, utter-still,
that, breaking, formed itself against the rocks
and slid into the main of light—we saw

there
beneath the burn of the horizon
a strange boat, entering the empty bay.

Williams recognized it: from Genoa!
A cry went up. Immediately
the women gathered at the upper porch,
gray-eyed, Mary pregnant,

already feasting on that future grief
devotion spares for the Cassandras of this world.

We hailed her as she cut a transverse course
for Lerici

and took possession there.
Two tons iron ballast and we have all summer.
Mary still ill-spirited, expected.
But soon it's finished. And she'll sail like a witch. I'll name her

Ariel.

3. *Annunciations in Time of Drought*

Mary, recalling.
Putney, 1839

Among the prayers and processions of relics,
all in want of rain, the heat
persisted. And we went on
spending our summer evenings on the water.

Care of the house was never-ending
with the sea coming up to the door. Mornings
I spent in the ilex grove
remembering an English garden.

The men had made a mistress
of the sea, built trysts upon a bark of reeds.
But I knew a single taper
can set the forest burning.

Something was growing inside me.
Presentiments. The estate's half-mad
proprietor had rooted up the ancient olives.
They tangled in my dreams

fleshlike, sinewy,
holding something from me. When I looked
the hillside gleamed
bare as a bone.

So days passed, without news or provisions.
And the people around us, savage.
My journal records nothing
May to June.

Only at night, the howls—wild
men among the rocks, their olive-
colored women lifting white
skirts to breed in the foam.

4. *Visions*

i.

Man is not a machine
Appearances belie
the heart's remorse

and joy
One suffers into truth
if one lives long enough

Anger
Jealousy
Unrest

grease the sockets of our eyes

ii.

Postage
from the limits
speaks of life beyond

the pale of one's affections
current interests
So far

to come to only this
knowledge
that breeds flies

Mind's self-devouring mind

iii.

Wing of night
hold for us
different visions

Our hollow bones
our flesh
a feathery wax

Morning warms
the waves' glass
all too clear

We soar outside ourselves

5. Postscript

My friends, my lovers now appear to me
mangled. Around them sweeps the sea

flooding the rooms, our house, our ruin.
Such was not my childhood vision.

Our boat is asleep on Serchio's stream,
Its sails folded like thoughts in a dream.

...

Mary has miscarried.

6. Lines

Gulf of Spezia
July 8, 1822

The sea is in its first night.
All day we watched the patterns mingle gold
leaf with azure of Italian light,

dissolve like dream in dream. We held
them buoyant on the surface of the eye
a brittle time. So much can be told.

A child will figure cloud shapes as they fly
from change to change; memory may keep
one against all others—a great tree,

its vaporous boughs and foliage rooted deep
in airy nothing, ramifying white.
Within that specter's shade the poet's sleep

is born. And what it will create—
what swarm of stars, what telescopic throng
filling the caverns of the mind, what

torchlight in the forests of the tongue—
remains as open to be seen
as is the sea, now, swelling like a sponge.

All through the welter of the afternoon
I watched a solitary cloud, a single seed
planted on the line of the horizon,

build into a mighty thunderhead,
thought's poplar, rooted in the salt sea wave,
at evening turn to autumn's darkest red,

red of remembered maples, or the grove
of sumac burning on the streams of Venice,
torches around us by the light it gave

as we, beneath the temples, palaces,
passed upon the waters' labyrinth
like spirits, edging to the gates of Dis.

But here, inside this light, no labyrinth.
The red sun glowered with a Cyclops eye
hurled shafts above us, shot its beams beneath

our keel. Gulf fathoms glistened. Italy
lay all behind us. All before us stood
the brilliant broken sepulcher of sky.

Thunder awoke us to the thrill of blood
too late, too late. The riggings' snap and snarl
was as our fibers, as the sea unmade

us. Now ten fathoms deep, the pearls
that were the eyes of Shelley, poet,
lie. Look at the phantom leaves their stare unfurls.

7. Dispellings

Three white wands
had been stuck in the sand to mark the poet's grave.

The elements
had done their work. We heaved

the body out, lime-eaten, indigo
against canary sand.

Along the blue smile of the bay
a line of surf, like teeth. Green flames

leapt to the oil and frankincense
and salt. The air full

of our oration, wave on wave,
tremulous with the pitch pine's sparks.

When it was finished,
jaw and heart remained.

The crowds had scattered.

The soldiers cooled the iron machine in the sea.

four

Clothing for the Transformation

for Rachel Parry

Walk on pampooties of fire-
red chili peppers. Wear

the boa's slough upon
your head, thought's skin.

Sedulous as Daedalus
fix into the wax

crow feathers for your gloves
lined with lizard sleeves.

Mold the plastron at your breast
from a loon's forsaken nest

trimmed with lichen, decked with turf
scooped from local earth. Enough.

Sleep. In the fleece of dreams
the beast to bear you onward comes.

Your shadow knocks. The veil you've spun
of homely cobwebs, put it on.

Voyager

We've packed our bags, we're set to fly
no one knows where, the maps won't do.
We're crossing the ocean's nihilistic blue
with an unborn infant's opal eye.

It has the clarity of earth and sky
seen from a spacecraft, once removed,
as through an amniotic lens, that groove-
lessness of space, the last star by.

We have set out to live and die
into the interstices of a new
nowhere to be or be returning to

(a little like an infant's air-borne cry).
We've set our sights on nothing left to lose
and made of loss itself a lullaby.

Song for the Interstices

Dismantlers of thresholds, lords
of the littoral where sea imagines stone,
absence of synapse in the thought
where anything is possible, idea's bone,

ink of Orion pressed upon
the cranial night the dark
honeycomb his mind's become,
hiatus of his heart's

desire, desire
of the wave to reach the rising Hunter's Moon:
Midnight. You there.
I here. The world between.

Nightcall. Going Nowhere

Somewhere at the end of this long New England night
near inland water, in an amber room
you sit at a window with the whole Wisconsin sky
gone indigo before you, and the stars.
The child at your lap sleeps on. She is
magnolia, onion blossom. At the brow,
the petal thin skin stirs like water
as a dream pulls past and settles.
She is beyond you, neither here nor there
but in-between drifts, buoyant on a breath
so slight it hardly startles
the gossamer that hangs between her lips.
She is no longer yours than you are mine,
the lines between us growing more remote
with every whistle of a wind

that catches at you now (you reach
and pull the window to and as you do
the autumn moon pulls over a green bay,
black fields, the cattails' bursting pods,
treefrogs that break their hearts apart to sing
the song of every godforsaken thing
dying to get beyond itself—)
                    Nightcalls. Going nowhere but inside
the festering backwaters of the brain,
thought-spawn, self-flagellants, a fecund moss
murky with recollection, marled with loss—
        the moon on oil-black water,
        its skim too thick to cast a star,
        at the heart a dark fin turning . . .

These are the things no one is going to touch,

the no-man-fathomed mockeries of sense
since, apparently, we've never learned to live
outside these bodies, since we lack
the spider's seeming infinite capacity
to trundle from its guts a living line—
these such stuff
as screams are made on—

forgive them. You will see that I am trying
to find a language fainter than the blue
of veins on eyelids sleeping,
a living line, to get to you,
almost a stranger, whom my heart
leans toward in ways I cannot own,
these signals of distress by which I cull
a bay, a field, an amber room
and hold you there, before the tie beam breaks,
before light gutters, or that infant wakes.

Pont du Loup

The lemon trees, in memory,
globes of sunlight on the manmade cliffs
and mountains, made as of an old man's dream
of love, its passage, a ravine of scars.

A house enclosed us, though it was not ours.
Enclosed your face in sleep. I watched
as embers ticked low signals to the stars
and a dog's bark coiled in scatterings.

I thought of our own passage. How we'd been
those years ago, before we owned a skin
between us, like a mirrored ghost
or sky on water mirroring.

At morning was the past:
the village with its famous bombed-out bridge,
high pillars littering the alpine gorge
bright-stitched with lemon trees.

Specimen

The glass lid closes. The Brazilian butterfly,
decadent in iridescent blues,
assumes a quieter and a stiller air
than the one through which our lonely bodies move
naked against each other, bone on bone,
nipple to nipple, limb locked over limb,
and turn till you lift over me as if in
flight, as if toward thoughts of taking flight—
your torso arced, your dreaming head thrown back,
I watch you move above me through the blue
tentative air of dusk as leaf to leaf,
petal to petal, the psyche reassumes
its dream of oneness in a single skin
I pull you taut across and hold you pinned.

Suppliant, Late April

To you, three sisters, I bring the bud, the branch, the thorn,
for the trees have recovered greenness.
I have no other reason.

All month—all century—the storms.
Word of a suicide. The body hung
three days unburied. The earth has broken open.

My love and I have lain as on
a precipice. Her fevered thoughts
have left the pillow torn.

By this green, let stem
your furies for a season,
O kindly ones.

Elegiac

The garden with its lurid statuary,
slant-eyed satyrs, the algal fountain babbling on
of metamorphoses, rumors of eternal
life in the cypress, its shade green to the bone:

I want you here, among these ruins
Time has left alone, the sundial
over us, innocently grown
ithyphallic in its sheath of ivy.

Duet

for Eva and Rohan

And had we fallen silent, had we stood
mute as two trees (the green meandering
of a vine between us, as of married thoughts)—
had we not opened up our ravaged throats
to the salutary light and air, saying

Yes to necessity that fells us all
in time, had we not grown
through grief or grievance into other skin
there is no saying what we might have been
but it would not be this, would not be song:

her body radiant with cancer, with its vision
of the end, her fluent bow
drawn its full length down across the string,
an oar through water; then, his following—
as wordless from our watchful shore, they row.

History

So. It happened. That was the way, was
how it was. Was how
we'd come to see it, viewed as through

display glass or diorama air, all
episodic, elsewhere—though we were
ourselves we looked at there, wide-eyed

faces averted from the might-have-how
into the ventricle of light we call
the now, the knowable, the urgent and

irrevocable tellable of how it was
we came here, happened on ourselves, just so
happened. Only just. But so.

Roman Room

Someday our buried life will come to this:
a shaft of sunlight touching the Etruscan
surfaces, the basin still intact
as if awaiting hands. How many

centuries sequestered is an expert's guess,
you tell me. I admire the tiles
some craftsman spiraled in the ceiling's dome
detailing Neptune's beard. Or someone's.

What will they say of us, who have no home,
we like to say, but one another? When they pry
our hearts apart and excavate the sum,
is that the place we'll lie? Where the words lie?

Covenant

This ring, made from the vertebra and rib
of the diamondback I found beneath the shed
coiled upon itself and ages dead
(the rattle hung above the empty crib),
is all the remnant of its brilliant skins.

Wear it in memory of our innocence.

Adam Unparadised

after Borges

The garden. Was it real? Was it a dream?
Long in the wandering light I have been asking,
as if in consolation, if the past
of this most miserable Adam weren't just

the fabrication of some god I dreamed.
Already imprecise in memory
my kingdom, that pellucid Paradiso,
but I know that it exists, and will persist,

if not for me. The unforgiving earth
is my inheritance, the incestuous wars
of Cains and Abels and their progeny.

Still. It must mean something to have loved.
To have been happy. To have lighted on
the living garden, if even for a day.

Notes

"Last Look": Most of the facts in this poem were culled from *Harper's* magazine, the monthly section titled "Findings."

"Caliban in After-Life": The epigraph comes from *The Tempest*, 5.1.275–76.

"Sea Change": Opening and closing lines, sections 1 and 7, are from Trelawny's *Recollections of the Last Days of Shelley and Byron* (London, 1858). Italicized lines, section 5, are from Shelley's "The Boat on the Serchio." Shelley's boat went down in the Gulf of Spezia, off the coast of Italy, July 8, 1822. When his body washed up, it was buried in a sandy grave; some days later it was exhumed by friends and burned in the Greek fashion. After the remains were brought to Rome, Trelawny had these lines from Shelley's "favourite play" inscribed on the tombstone: "Nothing of him that doth fade, / But doth suffer a sea change / Into something rich and strange."

"Nightcall. Going Nowhere": The phrase "no-man-fathomed" comes from Gerard Manley Hopkins's sonnet "No worst, there is none. Pitched past pitch of grief."

"Adam Unparadised": The title is Milton's, what he originally thought to call *Paradise Lost*. My adaptation of Borges's poem—titled (in English) "Adam Cast Forth"—owes a considerable debt in its phrasing to Alastair Reid's translation.